HOW T(

GRIEF AND LOSS

INTRODUCTION

What is grief? It is a normal but deeply painful response to loss. The most common loss is the death of a loved one; however, there are a lot of other changes in someone's life that involve losing something important which also results in grieving. No one is spared from loss or a feeling of grief; and the more significant the loss, the more intense the grief will be.

Different people have unique experiences with regards to loss, thus each handle grief differently. One person might take it all in stride and be back on track in a matter of months, but there are those that take too long to accept and to bounce back from grief.

After working with thousands of grievers, I have learned more and better ways to help people deal with grief. I am thrilled to be able to pass along what I have learned to make recovery more accessible and more possible for you.

As my personal stories illustrate, I did not come to our careers in grief recovery by way of intellectual pursuit. I am jolted into this work by our broken hearts. Every one of you arrives at this book because your heart has been broken too. While you already know your heart is broken, your question might be, "What do I do about it?" This book has the answer. The concepts of grief recovery presented here represent a breakthrough in helping grieving people deal successfully with loss.

Most professionals have addressed grief from a conceptual, intellectual perspective. This has often left grievers with much understanding— but very little recovery. This book focuses totally on recovery from the emotional pain caused by death, and other losses.

For all of you struggling with unresolved grief issues, I know that the actions outlined in this book will lead you to completion of the pain caused by loss. I also know that recovery is not an easy journey. I know that your losses may have closed your heart down. If I could, I would be with you as you take the actions that will lead your heart to open again. You may be afraid to start, or you may get scared along the way. Please remember that hundreds of thousands of people have used these same actions. I know that they join us in encouraging you to move through your apprehension and begin the process of recovery.

I wish you good luck on your journey.

Table of Contents

THE GRIEVING PROCCESS

The process immediately begins upon the sudden loss of a loved one. A person suffering from grief needs support from friends and family. The grief process can last differently for different people; it depends on the nature of the loss, the person's personality, and the amount and quality of support that the person is getting. The process may involve all or some of the following emotions:

Shock – The initial reaction to hearing news about losing someone is shock. This is a normal reaction. It is when the grieving person would feel an extreme numbness and disbelieve. It is during this stage that the people usually fail to make even the simplest of decisions; their minds are totally clouded, and they feel lost.

Suffering – There will be a feeling of suffering and it may take a long time before the grieving person would start to feel like his heart is starting to heal. There are a lot of other emotions that encompass suffering, like intense pain and hurt. There will also be a feeling of chaos and being disorganized. Daily routines are interrupted and those who are grieving tend to become anti-social, thinking that the people around them do not understand how they feel.

Anger – this feeling of anger comes from the feeling of being powerless to change the situation or to prevent the loss from happening. Sometimes it is also anger of being abandoned and left behind. In most tragic deaths involving fatal accidents and serious illnesses, there is anger towards the people who caused the accident and towards the doctors who failed to save the lives of their loved ones.

Guilt - this could also be felt for not having prevented the death or for not doing enough. There will be a lot of crying for people who grieve. Suffering can be the most difficult stage of grief because of the varying levels of emotions sufferers are subjected to. Their emotional stability is disrupted and there are those who will need professional help. It is during this stage that those who are grieving are in denial of their loss. Most of them have this feeling that if they sleep it off, thinking that everything will go away, and that it was all a bad dream. When they wake up and realize that it was not, they suffer some more; so acceptance is quite hard to come by.

Recovery – Acceptance will help guide the grieving person en-route to the recovery stage. During this stage, those who are grieving can start reorganizing their lives and restore some form of normalcy. Though, it will never be the same without the loved ones they've lost, they will have to accept that they have to carry on without them. There will be some bouts of loneliness during the process but it is normal since memories of the deceased will always remain. Obstacles Commonly Encountered During the Healing Stage

Grief can be brought about by plenty of other things besides death. One can grieve for the breakdown of a marriage or loss of a job. It can also be a result of losing your home due to a natural disaster. Sometimes, the healing process takes too long because of the refusal of the concerned people to seek help or to deal with their grief. There are people who get stuck in the denial stage that they have a hard time moving forward to acceptance and eventual healing.

While most people are quick to give comforting words such as, "you'll be fine" or "you have to stay strong", these are not really helpful according to expert psychologists. In fact, these words are rarely effective; as they can often mislead the sufferers so they end up denying their grief instead of handling it.

The best way to help people who are grieving is to encourage them to express what they feel. You cannot expect a grieving person to stay strong; he is at a very vulnerable stage right now and what he needs is a single moment of weakness and someone to support and to listen. He doesn't need people telling him to stay strong, because, frankly speaking, he cannot stay strong and he needs to let his feelings out instead of bottling them inside of him.

WHAT HAPPENED?

People who lost a loved one or experienced tragedy should be allowed to grieve. You are in a difficult situation right now, having lost someone dear to you, the pain could be overwhelming but you have to go through it. There will be a stage of denial, which is perfectly normal, but after that initial shock, you have to learn to embrace it in order for you to recover from it.

Trust the Grief

In your moment of despair, despite how painful it is, grief should be your "friend" because it will guide you on your way back to normalcy.

Three Major Points to Consider

•Every individual has their own unique way of expressing their grief. You have your own unique way of experiencing and expressing yours. As long as you do not get stuck in a negative emotion, you just continue to embrace grief.

•You are set to experience a roller-coaster ride of emotions. Grief does not have exact manifestations. It is unpredictable. There will be moments of silence and peace, and then you might experience a moment of almost reaching the breaking point. It is normal to cry; people in grief always need a good cry.

•Nothing is permanent in this world. You might be overwhelmed by grief today, but tomorrow is another day. You will eventually get over your loss. That's just the way it is.

In order to better cope with grief, it is important that you become aware of the different types of grief.

The death of someone you love is never easy. The extent of your grief depends on two major factors, including how deep your relationship with the person was, and the circumstances surrounding your loss.

The Three Types of Grief

Anticipatory Grief

This is when a loved one has been suffering from a long illness and then they finally died. The same kind of grief is felt when an elderly person dies. You somehow expected the outcome and you and the other members of the family prepared for its eventuality. However, even though it is expected, it is still painful. No matter how much one prepares for the death of a loved one, it will always be painful. But, having anticipated it, the members of the family wouldn't have a hard time dealing with grief, and the period of grieving is usually shorter.

Sometimes, when you have witnessed a loved one suffer long enough because of an illness; grief comes with a feeling of relief because you know that your loved one won't be feeling the pain of the illness anymore.

Sudden Loss

This type of grief is a complicated one because of the varying circumstances that surround the death of the loved one. It brings about an extreme feeling of shock because the suddenness of the death can be overwhelming. When loved ones meet tragic deaths, those who are left behind find it harder to deal with their loss and they grieve a lot longer.

Complicated Grief

This is the type of grief when the process doesn't take its normal course. The intensity of the pain and sadness combined take its toll on the person, most of the time reaching their breaking point. Those who are suffering from this type of grief find it hard to function the way they should, it's like they forgot how it felt like to be "normal". People who go through this kind of grief often end up developing depression and/or anxiety disorder.

Some deaths can be too traumatic for a person to experience. Some deaths that can cause complicated grief are those that resulted from violence or accident, murder, homicide, and suicide.

These deaths are hard to accept, especially the ones that were caused by another person. Most loved ones who were left behind find it hard to process the death of someone they love to heartless people, sometimes, people they don't know of.

A fatal accident resulting to death is also very devastating. The death of a child is also hard on parents.

While others come back from the experience, some get stuck. They would need professional help to resolve their grief.

STEPS TO HEALING A BROKEN HEART

Losing a loved one is devastating. There are no shortcuts to fixing a broken heart. Grief is a process that you have to go through in order to get complete healing. While things may never be the same again, you can still come back from the heartbreak and live your life again.

So to help you get on the right track, here are nine steps to complete healing:

1. **Admit that you're in a crisis**. Admit that you are hurting and it is okay to not be okay; it is actually normal in times like these. You shouldn't isolate yourself from your friends and family. The best way to recover is to spend time with them, even if you feel like being alone.

2. **Accept the pain**. As mentioned in the previous chapter, embrace grief, for you cannot hide from it anyway. Reality bites! People get heartbroken. If your marriage ends in divorce or if your spouse dies, it is something that you have to accept. Remember that nothing is permanent in this world. Losing something that mattered to you can be painful. Acceptance is an integral factor in your healing process.

3. **Change your thoughts**. The end of a relationship, the death of a loved one, or the loss of a job can be devastating. This could be the best time to change your frame of mind and look at things from a different perspective. You have to learn to bounce back from each fall. Look at the loss as an opportunity to find some time for yourself or to find a new career path.

4. **Learn to understand what you're feeling**. Get in touch with your emotions to better understand them. The feeling of extreme pain and sadness will never go away if you don't deal with them. The sooner you deal with them, the better you understand them. Go through the process. Feel the anger, the resentment, feel the pain, and feel the fear, even the shame. Take them all in. Once you've understood them, it will be easier to accept your loss.

5. **Believe that you deserve to be happy**. If you have lost a loved one to divorce, do not pity yourself; instead take this opportunity to improve yourself. Take some time off and just be happy.

If you have lost your job, just believe that if a door closes, you might find a window or another door that will open for you soon. Death is more difficult to accept because the loved one is gone forever but you have to face the music; you are still alive, so make your life matter.

6. **Learn some new things**. Take up a new hobby or a sport. When your mind is occupied, you have less time to feel sorry for yourself. Keep yourself occupied. The moment you become reclusive, it will take longer for you to recover.

7. **Keep a journal so you can write about what you feel**. You'll be surprised to find out how writing about what you feel helps you to talk to your own self. By writing them all out, you will begin to understand what you feel. Instead of venting your anger or sadness on other people, better channel them in a constructive way. When the most difficult times are over and you read them back, you'll be able to gain new insights. You'll learn how you were able to get past that difficult part of your life.

8. **Try to connect with the community or your local church.** Do volunteer works. The key is to not feel alone. Ask your local church for support groups you can join. Pain when shared with those who are in the same situation will be easier to bear.

9. **Go on a vacation**. Is there a place where you'd like to visit? If your parents live across the country, now is the best time to be with them.

You might have lost your one great love to death or divorce but that does not mean you cannot fall in love again. Consider the possibility of falling in love again. While you shouldn't force yourself to do so, it doesn't hurt to consider it as an option after a few years. Concentrate on yourself first and your journey to recovery. When the time is right it will happen.

MOVING ON

Once you have gone through the various stages of grief, moving on should become easier. By now, you are aware that there are different kinds of loss besides the death of a loved one, divorce, and job loss, which have been briefly discussed earlier. In addition, grief is also felt when you or a loved one is diagnosed of a fatal illness, a close friend or relative has to move away, and loss of ability or a limb.

Grief has many facets.

Here are some tips on how to move on:

•No one can go through that grief aside from you. No one, not even your closest friend or you parents can tell you how to handle grief. No one can tell what to feel. It is your sole responsibility.

•Grief has its own purpose. You need to go through the process so you can learn to accept everything that has happened. Losing someone or something important to you can be devastating but it is an experience where you can learn a lot from.

•Believe that this phase will be over soon. This is not a permanent feeling. Eventually you will heal and you will recover. No one gets stuck in sadness and emptiness forever.

•You have to take care of yourself. Grief can take its toll on your health and you might succumb to stress and anxiety. Dealing with a roller coaster of emotions while attending to arrangements can be stressful. Make sure that you take a break once in a while to recharge your energy.

•Take care of your health. Some people turn to food for comfort, it is referred to as emotional eating. This will not be good to your health and might result to obesity and other more serious medical conditions.

•Sharing your thoughts is good therapy. Whatever it is you are feeling, it is best if you talk to someone about it. When you talk with someone, it can somehow help ease your pain. People say that shared pain is easier to manage than the pain that you keep to yourself. Your friends and family will understand, so you just have to be honest about your true feelings.

•While it helps to be around your friends and family, it would also help if you find some time to be on your own. Why not take your family out for the weekend to somewhere you haven't been before, or you can travel alone. A vacation is a good way to ease stress.

•A loss can derail your route. It takes you away from your normal routine. Counselors say that it is best if you continue on with your normal activities. Do not alter what you usually do just because you are grieving. As much as possible, stick to your routines.

•It is perfectly all right to ask for help. Admitting that you are in pain is your first step to full recovery. Do not hesitate to ask for help because you cannot overcome this stage alone. It is okay to spend some time alone once in a while, but do not isolate yourself. The people around you will understand that you cannot be self-sufficient at this stage. Let the people who want to help you do their part.

•While it is good to learn new things and explore other options, now is not the best time make major decisions and extreme life changes. Wait until you have restored a sense of balance into your life before making life altering decisions and/or ventures. Do not make decisions in spur-ofthe-moment situations; you might regret them in the long run.

•Grief is a process. You don't overcome pain and recover in just weeks or months. Some people even take them years to fully recover. Do not rush into it; you need to process your feelings to better handle them.

•Keep in mind that grief may be painful but it cannot harm. It is a very difficult situation but you will soon survive and when you look back, you will just smile at how you were able to handle grief.

•Do not regret anything. Your marriage might have ended in divorce but think about how happy you were before the split and if you have kids, they are your best rewards.

•Do not be surprised if you regress a little during the process. It is a normal thing when you are going through the process. Trust that it will not last long.

•It is okay to be reminded of the anniversary. Deaths are painful and whenever anniversaries happen, all the more that you will feel the pain of your loss.

FINDING PEACE

AT SOME POINT IN OUR LIVES, EACH OF US HAS EXPERIENCED moments of calm fulfillment, moments when everything seemed "okay," when our instinctive trust in the Universe came to the surface and we let down our guard and our defenses. We felt warmth, we felt peace, we felt contentment. We breathed in deeply, our abdomens unusually relaxed, our shoulders uncharacteristically low. We breathed out a long, liberating exhale. "Aaaahhhhhhhhh." The subtle fear was gone. The wariness had melted. The confusion and doubt had receded into irrelevance. We felt connected. We felt complete. We felt whole.

Some would say it felt like being in our mothers' arms, or back in the womb. Some would say it felt like a sense of "oneness" with nature or with the Universe. Some would say they forgot all their cares and just "let go." Some would say it's the experience we were born for—the "peace that passeth all understanding."

For a mother, it may have come through the experience of childbirth, of bringing another human being into the world. For others it may have come through romance. Or through a winning athletic effort or an outstanding artistic performance. Perhaps it came through scuba diving, skydiving, a scientific breakthrough, sex, mountain climbing, or just sitting by a stream or on the beach. It may have come at the moment we fell in love, or at the moment we lay in the grass staring up at the stars in the nighttime sky. It may have come in meditation or prayer, that evening in Paris, the gondola ride in Venice, the picnic in Central Park, being caressed and kissed by a school of fish while snorkeling, on the motorcycle ride down Pacific Coast Highway, in the moment he said, "I love you."

At these moments, we transcend our limitations. And the state of expansiveness we move into is love. Since we have no fear, we have no anger because the two are intricately intertwined. When we're "in love," even people we don't like are suddenly okay. We may feel compassion for their predicament. There's no attraction to negativity because it separates and divides, and we are so content in our experience of merging.

But that very recognition, when the mind begins to focus on it, is terrifying. We've let down our defenses. We think, My God, I've allowed myself to be vulnerable. I am unprotected. I am out of my mind! Come back to earth. Get hold of yourself. Come to your senses. And suddenly we are again separate and frightened.

We return to the comfortable familiarity of our fears. We sacrifice bliss and joy and aliveness to feel "safe." For a moment our minds quieted and our hearts opened and we expanded into larger, less defined beings, with a spirit of playfulness and freedom. But as soon as our minds "kicked in," they told us we were in unsafe territory.

Later, we remember the experience and we desperately want to recapture it. But the problem is that we are using our minds to create the experience again ... and our minds want to come along this time. We want the bliss, but we also want the "safety" of our judging minds.

So we become addicted to whatever the method was that got us into that state of expanded awareness in the first place. We want to do it all the time. And if it was other people who got us there, we want to be with them all the time, and to protect them and ensure that they won't fall into danger ... or the arms of another.

Our grief is the agony that is generated by this effort to control. It's the conceptualizing of a "perfect" Universe—one in which everything and everyone is just as we want—and then the resistance to the way things and people really are.

If we think back on our moments of bliss and contentment, we would very likely remember that they came unexpectedly, not as a result of something we had designed for ourselves, but as a result of a surprising development, an unforeseen turn of events and emotions. We may have practiced our golf swing for years, but the day we first broke eighty on the golf course our feelings of intense satisfaction were experienced not so much as the "end result" of all our preparation, but rather as a magical unlocking of the doorway to fulfillment inside us that had previously been sealed shut.

Similarly, when we "fall in love" the feeling often washes over us at an unexpected moment. It is a "high" unlike any we've ever felt. And though the physical and mental images of our beloved are connected to the unfolding of the experience, that experience is still inside of us.

The foundations of our grief are built in our minds' misperception that the experience of love was fed into us from outside—that we can only have it if the people who triggered it are present in our lives in the way we want them to be, or the circumstances of our lives are exactly as we have designed them in our minds.

We don't acknowledge how vulnerable we are ... we want things the way we want them. We don't recognize the improbability of our lives—and the people in them—working out the way we want them to. It is almost as if we constantly climb up a tree on the edge of a cliff, make our way out to a thin, fragile branch that overhangs the canyon, jump up and down on that skinny, fragile branch, and then shout out, "I'm going to be really upset if this branch breaks and I fall into the chasm."

In so many ways, we construct the conditions of our own suffering and then, when the suffering comes, we feel victimized by some outside force, or power, or individual.

Sometimes the grief in a relationship comes because a state of love, acceptance, and fulfillment was never achieved. Many of us have had extremely difficult relationships with our parents. If that is the case, our lives come to revolve, often subconsciously, around the process of attempting to resolve and complete whatever conflicts and incompleteness exist in those relationships.

It is possible and even common for an individual to spend an entire lifetime in a profound state of discontent, driven by an emptiness that dates back to some slight, some series of slights, or some offense that one or the other parent committed during the child's early years. A woman may spend her entire adult life habitually, mechanically sleeping with man after man after man all because her "inner child" longs for a love, affection, and acceptance she never got from her father.

And a man may spend decades amassing a fortune but never achieving happiness because he is driven to disprove a father who told him he would "never amount to anything." At some level, no matter how much money he has, he still fears that he "doesn't amount to anything." It is equally plausible that the same man might spend every day of his adult life sitting in barrooms and consuming quarts of Jack Daniels all because he believed his father.

Our grief may also arise out of the awareness, real or imagined, that we have lost the possibility of having a good relationship because of age, illness, or being physically challenged. And if our sense of meaning in life has arisen from our ability to produce and achieve, the process of retirement may bring on a profound experience of grief as we wrestle with a loss of identity and direction.

It's as if we don't know who we are or what life means if we aren't in constant motion. For years, I have carried around a full-page ad I cut out of a magazine. It's an ad for Rolls Royce Motor Cars. It features a photograph of two cars stopped at a traffic light in Beverly Hills. One is a $90,000 BMW and the other is a $250,000 Rolls Royce.

The very well-dressed man behind the wheel of the BMW is looking longingly at the Rolls Royce. The caption reads, "Rolls Royce ... Quite

Simply the Best Motor Car in the World." But I have always felt the caption should be, "It's Never Enough."

Over the course of my life, I have had the opportunity to know and spend a lot of time with some very wealthy people. And, in most circumstances, the old clichés hold true. Money does not buy happiness. I know some extremely wealthy people who are extremely confused and miserable. And it is never enough. Most people in the world are convinced that if they had more money, their worries would disappear. But people who have money suffer from an extraordinary fear of losing it; or worrying that it's not enough, that they need more and more and more to keep pace with inflation and to avoid suffering embarrassment as their friends, neighbors, and associates ascend higher and higher.

We look with awe upon those people in our society who we define as "driven." We admire them and compare ourselves to them, often wishing that we could cultivate the same level of "ambition" and dedicate ourselves to the same degree of accomplishment.

While it is possible to be single-mindedly devoted to a cause for humanitarian or philanthropic reasons or for the fulfillment of some personal dream or vision, more often people who are "driven" are motivated by some deep inner turmoil and sense of emptiness. Their manic drive to achieve and accomplish really grows out of a need to relieve their own inner discontent—their grief—in much the same manner as those of a different temperament might be inclined to drink their troubles away. Substance abuse and addiction, sexual addiction, power addiction, money addiction—all of these are expressions of unresolved grief, of a profound sense of loss and incompleteness.

I don't mean to suggest that there is no value in hard work. Nor do I mean to suggest that we shouldn't, at times, dedicate ourselves with a one-pointed focus toward the accomplishment of some heart-felt dream or the realization of some extremely meaningful personal goal. Hard work, discipline, and the ability to be focused are essential, invaluable tools for accomplishing one's life purpose, for leading a life that feels "full" and "meaningful" rather than "empty." The irony is that only through discipline can we achieve freedom.

One of the greatest griefs we can experience is the sense that we did less than we were capable of—in our relationships, in our world, and in our efforts to accomplish whatever our hearts encouraged us to accomplish. Simply stated, when we die or a loved one dies, as we reflect on our lives, or our relationships, we are usually much less concerned about what we did than about what we didn't do. On the other hand, as has been stated so often in recent years, when we are on our deathbeds we are usually not wishing we had spent more time at the office.

The key is to find a balance, to find fulfillment in everything we do rather than to "sleepwalk" through life neglecting things and people important to us, mindlessly striving for an elusive sense of "success" and "achievement." Responsible, focused management of finances can eliminate much of the debilitating stress that surrounds financial hardship. It is not evil to make money, and it is wise to save it. But the "drive" we see in many people often arises out of less healthy, less conscious motives.

In general, everything our culture has told us and taught us about grief has exacerbated the problem rather than relieve it. In order to "heal" through this experience, we must unlearn much of what we learned about dealing with grief. Rather than pushing it away, rather than pretending it's not present, rather than keeping a stiff upper lip, we need to have the courage to cry, to sob, to open our hearts and allow ourselves to experience the pain, the rage, the frustration, the anger, the profound sadness. We need to know that we will not drown in it all. We may go under for a while, but we won't drown if we stay connected to our hearts.

Our hearts are our lifelines. If we react in fear and close them, we lose the healing potential and solace they offer. Our hearts have no boundaries—they are infinite. The only boundaries they have are the ones our minds impose on them.

The healing of grief begins when we allow our hearts to be open and vulnerable, when we allow ourselves into them, and allow our wounds and sorrows to be healed by them. While our cultural conditioning has been to close our hearts at times of sadness or fear, the true healing takes place when we open them to absorb our darkness, and swallow it into the infinite light they contain.

The miracle is that our very own hearts offer us the opportunity for growth, for completeness, for forgiveness, for nurturing, and for the realization of infinite opportunities. Real fulfillment is found inside ourselves. It isn't dependent on the presence of, or actions of, anyone else. It isn't dependent on the acquisition of material possessions and wealth. Each loss, each place of emptiness, each unresolved grief, each resentment, and each failure can be healed in the infinite mercy of our own hearts.

HOW TO TURN LOSS INTO HEALING

When a loved one dies, a relationship ends, or a powerful desire is not fulfilled, we have lost something or someone external to ourselves. We think our lives will forever be incomplete. We allow ourselves to believe that our inner happiness and our capacity to love are dependent on individuals and circumstances we have no ability to control. But the route through the sadness is to dive deeper into our own hearts, our own souls, our own intuitive trust.

Loss enters our lives in a variety of ways. Some losses come suddenly, unexpectedly, with no opportunity to prepare, no ability to say good-bye, no chance to say what was left unsaid or to do what was left undone.

Others losses come over time, perhaps through a prolonged illness, where the opportunities to "finish business" and "say good-bye" have been set against a backdrop of physical and emotional suffering; the body and sometimes the mind of a loved one slowly deteriorate until they are no longer suitable vehicles to hold the being we loved. The relationship may end abruptly or linger on in a state of "near death" for years.

Because our culture has, historically, given us precious little preparation for these inevitable experiences, at the moment a loved one dies or a relationship ends or we are told we're terminally ill, we often feel like we've crashed into a brick wall. We're confused and frustrated. We're shattered.

We're dazed. We keep replaying the facts in our minds, desperately searching for some misunderstanding, some mistake, some missing piece that makes the reality turn out to be as unreal as we feel in our hearts it must be. The mind says, This just simply couldn't have happened. I can't imagine my life without ... And yet, when those we love have died or have left us, each morning we wake and once again face the reality that they are physically gone. At times, we have to remind ourselves. It's as if we subconsciously hoped that the new dawn would bring a new reality, would rewrite history and erase the tragedy. If we have lost loved ones through separation or divorce, we struggle to comprehend that which seems unthinkable, to expiate our horror that those we loved have chosen to leave us. At times that is even more painful than dealing with their physical deaths.

In either case, there are moments when we feel their presence within us. We hear their voice. We smell their perfume. We see them vividly in our mind's eye. We can almost feel their touch. We feel the way we would if they were here. But our intuitive, emotional sense of connection with

them is at odds with our rational knowledge that they are gone. We are inclined to dismiss our sense of
connection with them because we have no cultural context in which to understand it.
If we are working with a terminal disease in our own bodies, we have moments when we "forget" and, for whatever short period of time, we come out from under that dark cloud. And if we sense that we may have participated in the onset of the disease, as we might with certain forms of cancer, heart disease, cirrhosis, or AIDS, we face the guilt and confusion of having lived our lives with ambivalence. We question why we consciously engaged in behaviors that might have hastened life's end.

Each day we make decisions about how to deal with these realities. We may approach the pain and the confusion a little bit at a time, step-by-step as the days go by, responding to some deep intuitive understanding that our ability to live life fully will either be enhanced or diminished by the degree of honest awareness we can bring to these events.

We may notice that our cultural training, which has been to ignore, deny, and avoid whatever is unpleasant, leads us deeper into confusion and numbness by offering only distraction as a solution. We may also notice that the relentless effort of our minds to "understand" what has happened in some subtle way keeps the raw edge on our pain. We are caught in the agonizing despair of our grief because we continually attempt to use our minds to resolve it, or to help us ignore it. But the real healing of grief can't take place until we make the journey from the mind to the heart. And when the heart is broken, the thought of reentering it is terrifying. But, the heart is precisely where the healing takes place. And when it is broken, it is also wide open.

For more than twenty-five years, I have made it a practice to visit with, explore with, and at times care for people who are terminally ill. I also have spent a great deal of time intuitively navigating the sometimes stormy, sometimes fog-shrouded waters of grief—my own and that of many others. Often in the course of social conversation when I tell people that I spend time sitting at the bedsides of people who are dying and holding the hands of people in grief, the response is one of shock bordering on horror. "Oh my God! How do you do that? That must be so depressing!" At an earlier time in my life, I would have reacted the same way. But at some point, because I had the opportunity to confront death so many times, I began to get the sense that in teaching us to avoid the unpleasant and encouraging us to deny the inevitable, our culture has robbed us of many, many precious opportunities to gain a deeper, more immediate sense of who we are and what our lives are all about.
We search desperately for meaning in life. We want to know that it all adds up to something, that we are not just random events in a trivial,

uncaring, meaningless Universe. Intuitively, we sense that there must be something very profound about such an infinitely complex and intricate world.

But our cultural training encourages us to perceive the events of our lives and our world through a selective viewfinder. We always seek to filter out whatever is unpleasant. And yet, here it is inside us. And there it is around us. By diverting our eyes, our minds, and our awareness from so much of what exists in our environment, by pretending that aging, decay, danger, and death are best dealt with through avoidance and ignorance, we have short-circuited our ability to fully experience what it is to be human. At the same time, we have cut off access to the parts of our beings that would be most helpful in times of emotional, spiritual, and existential crisis. We need only look at the widespread drug and alcohol abuse in our culture to realize that we are extremely unskilled at working with confusion, pain, and suffering. Most of us only know how to medicate and numb ourselves. We haven't got a clue about how to turn and face the demons that we think are tormenting us.

A number of years ago Ram Dass said to me, "If you want to get really high, try living in Truth." For a long time I pondered the meaning of that statement. And slowly, primarily through the frequent interaction with grief and dying, I began to see that Truth has extraordinary power. That looking directly at what is is tremendously transformative. That every time we divert our eyes, every time we pretend that the people, places, and events of our lives are other than they are, we diminish our capacity to be whole beings. We subtly give ourselves the message that our hearts and minds are too small, too finite, too limited to handle the Universe and all of its infinite beauty and seemingly infinite horror.

So now I can share with you the certainty that dealing with grief and loss need not be depressing. In fact, it can be some of the most inspirational, uplifting, and meaningful work of a lifetime.

As Don Juan said to Carlos Casteneda in Journey to Ixtlan:

Death is our eternal companion ... an immense amount of pettiness is dropped if your death makes a gesture to you, or if you just have the feeling that your companion is there watching you.

When a loved one is ill or has died, or we face a potentially terminal illness of our own, or we deal with divorce or separation, we are pushed beyond the boundaries our minds have created to maintain the illusion of safety, continuity, stability, and control. Our defenses crumble. We simply have no energy to support them. We are

thrust into an uncomfortable realm of confusion and
apprehension. The ways in which we have known and experienced our lives, our loved ones, and ourselves are in disarray.
It is—amazingly enough—an extremely ripe moment. It is a time when we have the opportunity to break free of the prisons in our minds that have held us back from fully immersing ourselves in life. It is a time to let go of pettiness and pretense.
No, working with grief and dying does not have to be depressing. Of course, it can be exhausting if the care of loved ones involves demanding around-the-clock duties, little sleep, extraordinary effort to relieve suffering, meticulous attention to the minute details of medication, and so on. And it can be difficult if, no matter what is done, the loved ones' condition continues to worsen or they and their families ride the roller coaster of positive reports and improvement, followed by negative reports and backsliding, followed by more improvement, followed by more worsening ... But it does not have to be depressing.

Working with grief and dying is difficult and exhausting when denial and aversion are present because the psychological and emotional effort required to push away Truth can completely sap the energy of everyone involved. It is not the illness, or the death, or the loss, or the grief that causes our suffering. It is our attempt to push it all away that causes our suffering. When we face it all openly and honestly, exploring the depths and subtleties of what loss, grief, and death have to teach us, the process can become profound. Sometimes it can even be humorous. At times, it even becomes joyous.

I do not mean to discount or trivialize the tremendous physical and emotional challenges that can be part and parcel of dying and loss. But it doesn't have to be an unrelieved tragedy.

Over many years I have learned that even the greatest tragedies in life can become the groundwork for tremendous growth and insight. Profound loss can be the catalyst for the shedding of old skin, the loosening of rigidity. Profound loss can pave the way for a new aliveness, a new enthusiasm, a totally new awareness.
I have seen dozens of people work with tragic and painful loss, with things so horrifying they seem completely unworkable. And slowly, eventually, many of those people come to a resolution of their feelings. In an astonishing number of cases, it's almost as if their lives have been strangely enhanced by an experience they wouldn't have wished on their worst enemies. Would they choose not to have had the experience? In most cases, yes. But the fact is they did have it, and they made a decision to work with what the Universe put on their plates, no matter how distasteful it may have been.

If I were to briefly summarize what leads to a growthful resolution of grief, I would say that instead of clinging to our models of how it should have been, or how we wish it was, we simply turn and look at life, as it is.

Conclusion

Once the initial reaction of shock and denial, there comes a whole lot of other emotions. One is anger and a feeling of hopelessness for not having control over things. Anger at the people who caused the loss. Then, depression and sadness set in. When you are able to understand your emotions and why you are feeling that way you are feeling, you will be on your way to resolution and recovery.

• Putting into words, your fears, thoughts, and feelings is a good therapy. It is another way of acknowledging the pain as you go through it.

• Do not isolate yourself. You need support and the people around you are willing to give you that. Reconnect with friends and family. Join support groups in your church or community.

• Participate in a new sport or hobby. Volunteer in one of your church's outreach activities.

• Go on vacation. Have some alone time.

•Accept your grief. It is okay to admit that you are in pain and that you need help.

•Create new opportunities. Remember that if God closes a door, He will surely open a window.

•Get in touch with your spiritual side. Take a sabbatical. Attend retreats for spiritual renewal.

•Do not worry. Let the normal grieving process take its course. No need to rush, you will get there eventually.

Thank you for taking the time to read and practice the steps provided to you in this book. I can assure you that if you practice what is taught here, you will learn to embrace and grow from your grieving experiences.

I will also like to ask you for a quick favor. I like to provide my readers with great reading experiences and extremely valuable content so, if you have enjoyed reading this book and believe that is has been of help you I will greatly appreciate your kindness by leaving a review on amazon.

I will now like to wish you luck and many moments of immense happiness to your life.

-Alexis Valentino